Endorsements

Seldom do we experience epochal times like we are in now. God is faithful to raise up men and women who strategically release prophetic direction which opens up navigation pathways through the morass of confusion and resistance. Clay Nash is one of these men for our now time. A prophet, a man of integrity, a family man and one with great courage; a man who knows God! I know of no one personally who has the degree of depth, insight and direction in his dreams that Clay does. I pay attention to what this man dreams. A must book for a NOW time!

Barbara J. Yoder
Lead Apostle, Shekinah
Regional Apostolic Center

*****

The Hebrew prophet, Joel, quoted by the apostle Peter on the day of Pentecost, declared:

In the last days, God says, I will pour out of My Spirit on all mankind (all flesh) and your sons and daughters shall prophesy, and your young men shall see visions, and your old men shall dream dreams...

Acts 2:16-17

The Spirit of God connects generations, i.e., young men and old men; and they both hear from heaven. The young man's vision is a better version of the old man's dream because there is progress in the Kingdom of God moving forward. As King Jesus sits upon the throne, the Spirit of God will be poured out, and heaven will communicate the will of God for the earth!

The dreams the Spirit has given apostle Clay Nash powerfully connect the current proceeding revelatory word of the Lord from the throne with the Scriptures!

Dreams, (as well as visions), inspire and instruct the body of Christ to step up as The

Ekklesia Army, which is the Kingdom Government of the enthroned Christ on the earth that wields authority in the heavens and on the earth. We, the Ekklesia, must step up in every way so that the purposes and plans of the Lord God are implemented in every sphere of life: personal, societal, cultural, and political.

Dreams (and visions) from the Lord will lead us into intensive intercession, declaration, and Kingdom decrees. Dreams from the Spirit can heal individuals and nations! They can also make us more aware and alert to the ministry of angels working and warring on our behalf.

On a personal note, I am delighted at the frequent appearances of Dr. Dutch Sheets in Clay's book. Dutch is one of my spiritual sons. We have walked together for over forty years. This volume underscores the significance of Dutch's ministry as a major leader in the Prayer Movement and in the 3rd Great Awakening Movement.

In this critical and chaotic hour in our nation's history, we need this book more than ever!

Jim Hodges

*****

One cannot read the Bible without noting the mention of dreams and visions throughout the holy scriptures. In the Book of Numbers, chapter 12:5-6, it is written that God appeared in a cloud and said these words:

> *Then the Lord came down in a pillar of cloud; he stood at the entrance to the tent and summoned Aaron and Miriam. When the two of them stepped forward, he said, "Listen to my words: When there is a prophet among you, I, the Lord, reveal myself to them in visions, I speak to them in dreams."*

Using God's own words, when there is a prophet among you, he reveals himself to that person in visions and speaks to them in dreams:

Clay Nash. I have known Clay Nash for several years now through our shared hope that the United States of America would live up to our national motto "In God We Trust."

I am certain that *God Dreams to Make America Great Again* will bless you. As we enter the last of the Last Days, I am confident that the ministry and gifts of Clay Nash are being used by God to lead and prepare Christians around the world. I am proud to be a friend to a man of God and patriot like Apostle Clay Nash."

> Sen. Jason Rapert
> Founder & President of the National
> Association of Christian Lawmakers
> Lead legislative sponsor of the 2013
> Arkansas Heartbeat Protection Act and
> 2015 Arkansas Ten Commandments
> Monument Act.

*****

Hear now My words If there is a prophet among you, I, the Lord, shall make Myself known to him in a vision. I shall speak with him in a dream"

Numbers 12:6

There are prophets among us, and the Lord is releasing an amazing number of dreams through His servants. One of those whom the Lord is using is Apostle Clay Nash. In this timely release, *God Dreams to Make America Great Again*, Clay shares his dreams and the dreams of others that are giving clarity, direction and strategy to the people of God that will cause the release of the divinely appointed destiny of our nation – the United States of America.

Dr. Tom Schlueter, Pastor
Prince of Peace House of Prayer
Texas Apostolic Prayer Network
Coordinator

*****

God Dreams to Make America Great Again is an adventurous prophetic journey that reveals God's heart for this nation. This book is about a "go-to" kingdom leader with a keen awareness of spiritual reality, expertise and experience in revelation, and a lifetime of integrity as God's representative.

On our journey together, we encounter many facets of faithfulness, such as God revealing key strategic places and people as well as decisive words that decree His heart. However, on this expedition, we also run into the deepest darkness--what God knows we must overcome to produce a kingdom victory.

This book reveals the brightest lights in the darkest tunnels. I like this book because it has the most mature handling of prophetic dreams, history's prepared pioneers running with assignments, and encounters with breakthrough spiritual technologies of hope, mercy, miracles, and prophetic wonder.

God does indeed dream and causes us to dream with Him about making America great again!

Dr. Don Lynch, Apostle
Freedom House Kingdom Center,
Jacksonville, Florida

*****

Apostle Clay Nash's book of dreams, interpretations and decrees is the book of the hour. Never before has anyone compiled such a cutting-edge document that can and will be used to save this nation. I urge everyone to get a copy of this book and speak the dreams, interpretations and decrees contained within it by faith. This will be the source of President Trump's re-election and the Spiritual Awakening of America!

Dr. Dwain Miller
Senior Pastor of Cross Life Church of
Little Rock

My friend Apostle Clay Nash, has a long history of flowing in a realm of the prophetic that includes dreams. And his book, *God Dreams to make America Great Again* is essential reading for these un-precedented times. While our nation is navigating through treacherous waters, many who should be helping are attempting to sink it. But God has a plan and is releasing many dreams with remarkable & specific revelation so that we can partner with Him. Therefore, we must glean the insight and foresight that these dreams offer so that we can align our prayers, decrees, and activities accordingly. Just as importantly, hope is revived and faith strengthened when we see in a God-given dream that His dream is to make America great again.

Apostle David Hertel
Hope Fellowship Church
Brandon, MS

*****

From the beginning, God has used dreams as signposts to light the way for His people. A deep sleep fell upon Adam in the garden of Eden and from his side God formed his destiny. Jacob slept with his head on a rock and saw a ladder at the gate to heaven where angels traveled. God still sends revelations of man's future and destiny through dreams and visions today. Clay Nash is a prophet chosen by God to climb this dream ladder where angels walk to receive signposts from God that point us to our destiny. I thoroughly endorse Clay and his dream revelations.

Mary Glazier
President of Windwalkers International
Co-founder of Kingdom Alliance Network

*****

The word of God tells us that without a vision a people perish. Friends, this book will give the prophetic vision that is key for our nation in this new era. This compilation of dreams, visions and prophetic insight provides clear direction to what God is saying in this hour concerning America. These rhema words will bring hope, encouragement, faith and empowerment to contend and intercede in agreement with the now spoken word of the Lord to see His Kingdom plan manifest in this strategic, now time. *God Dreams to Make America Again* is must read for all believers. Truly, the best is yet ahead. Thank you, Clay, for scribing His words and dreams for our nation and empowering the Ekklesia to arise in this hour to see Kingdom history unfold.

Rebecca Greenwood
Christian Harvest International
Strategic Prayer Apostolic Network
Author of: *Authority to Tread, Destined to Rule, Glory Warfare, Discerning the Spirit Realm*

*****

God Dreams to Make America Great Again will usher you into the very heart of God's redemptive plan for America. The Lord said that this book is a "War Chest"!

Historically, a war chest referred to the chest located in the homes or barracks of soldiers, in which the soldier kept arms, armor and money to be opened in time of war.

We are in a war for the destiny of the United State of America. Clay Nash has provided us with a strategic weapon and resource that will awaken, empower and equip you with an arsenal of decrees to establish God's Kingdom plan and purpose in your city, state and our nation.

Let Holy Spirit transport you into the war room of heaven and access this incredible war chest of dreams, interpretations and decrees. The war chest is open!

Betty Love
President Love Ministries, Inc.,
Miracle City Global

Jesus said, "Hear what Holy Spirit says to the church." Dreams are one of the ways He activates revelation, enlightenment, and strategies. Apostle Clay Nash is one of God's prophetic dreamers. I have been blessed and instructed by the godly dreams given to my friend and co-laborer in the Gospel of Christ many times, and so will you.

This book is so strategic. Read it. Pray it. Meditate on the dreams of men and women of God he has searched out. You will hear what Holy Spirit is saying in one of our world's most defining moments.

Dr. Tim Sheets
Apostle, Author
Tim Sheets Ministries

*****

Dreams and visions have always been the beacon of hope for a nation. Dreams are the moment when God turns the tide and a clear way is shown. The vision of Moses led the children of Israel out of Egypt. The dreams of Joseph saved the lineage of Abraham, Isaac and Jacob. Isaiah saw the Lord and received a calling to a nation. God has given Clay dreams that I believe will help turn the tide of America. It is a great honor that I recommend this book.

Ken Malone
Forerunner Ministries, Florida

*****

When my friend Clay Nash told me he was writing this book, my heart leaped. Because of Clay's rich history with God through dreams, I knew that God's hand was moving mightily throughout our nation.

We face harrowing times and conditions that man alone cannot resolve or even endure. Thank God for His divine providence in making America great and the world great. We are first and foremost sons and daughters of the King of Kings. Through our prayers and supplication, we bring our individual nations under the authority of the Kingdom of God and walk in His blessings.

Yes, God does have a dream for America, and He wants you to be a part of it. If you are hungry for the restoration of a godly America, read this book, consume the prophetic dreams it contains, and be equipped by one of the best persons I know regarding dreams and God's heart for the healing of our nation.

God bless America.

Will Ford
Co-Author of *The Dream King: How the Dream of Martin Luther King Jr. Is Being Revealed to Heal Racism In America.*
www.dreamstreamco.com

*****

What an honor it is to know and co-labor in the Kingdom of God with Clay and Susan Nash. Over ten years ago, God orchestrated through some amazing ways for us to connect and ultimately align for His purposes. My life, and the purposes of God through the ministries that I lead, have never been the same, and I am forever grateful.

Over these years, I have seen Clay develop from an incredibly gifted and anointed prophet and apostle into a seasoned, accurate voice for the Lord in this New Era that clearly and consistently releases the grace of the Lord, the authority of the Father, and the empowerment of Holy Spirit. Clay faithfully stewards the dreams, prophetic encounters and unlocking of Kingdom revelation that Holy Spirit gives him with humility, clarity, and boldness.

As I have walked with Clay and Susan quite closely over these last ten years, I can confidently say that their lives are marked by a deep and genuine relationship with the Lord that is lived out in authenticity and honor for the Lord, each other, and those they meet along life's path. Those who chose to partake of what God releases through Clay's words of counsel, wisdom, and revelation greatly benefit and are strengthened for the journey of faith.

I highly encourage you to glean all that you can from the pages of dreams, interpretations, and prayer declarations contained within this book. Don't just read it. Study it. Meditate on it with your Bible close at hand. Ask Holy Spirit to unlock and deposit in your heart wisdom, revelation, and understanding of the ways of the Kingdom and God's original intent for our Nation. Then boldly pray along with all the rest of us who are burning with holy passion to see what God dreams for America to come to fullness in our day and in the years to come.

For His glory alone,
Jacquie Tyre
City Gate, Atlanta GA

God Dreams
to Make
America Great
Again

by

Clay Nash

God Dreams to
Make America Great Again

by Clay Nash

Copyright © 2020 by Clay Nash

Unless otherwise indicated, all scripture is from the NASB, taken from the New American Standard Bible, © 1960, 1962, 1963, 1968, 1971, 1972, 1973, 1975, 1977, 1995 by the Lockman Foundation.

ISBN: 978-0-9835857-8-7

Editing/Layout by Jim Bryson
(JamesLBryson@gmail.com)

Graphics by David Little Munoz

Table of Contents

Dedication

I dedicate this book to my Savior, Lord and King Jesus Christ. I thank You for reaching down and pulling me from the pit and setting my feet on a firm foundation and putting a new song in my mouth—a song of praise to you.

I also dedicate this book to Susan, my wife of over 47 years, my helpmate and the greatest friend I have ever known. Susan, thank you for always trusting and believing in me to the point of allowing me to be the risk-taker I am.

I cannot stop there for I would not be true to my heart.

I further dedicate this amazing work to Jim Bryson, an editor, ghostwriter, publisher, a man of miraculous ability to finish this book in 10 days, and most of all, my friend. Jim, thank you for your willingness to draw out of me what God has put in me.

Foreword by Dutch Sheets

Then Zerubbabel the son of Shealtiel and Jeshua the son of Jozadak arose and began to rebuild the house of God which is in Jerusalem; and the prophets of God were with them supporting them.

Ezra 5:2

And the elders of the Jews were successful in building through the prophesying of Haggai the prophet and Zechariah the son of Iddo. And they finished building according to the command of the God of Israel and the decree of Cyrus, Darius, and Artaxerxes king of Persia.

Ezra 6:14

They rose early in the morning and went out to the wilderness of Tekoa; and when they went out, Jehoshaphat

1

stood and said, "Listen to me, O Judah and inhabitants of Jerusalem, put your trust in the Lord your God and you will be established. Put your trust in His prophets and succeed."

2 Chronicles 20:20

I'm baffled as to why the Church thought for so long it could function—or that God would want them to function—without His prophetic gift. Second Chronicles 20:20, quoted above, tells us to believe the prophets, which would also mean acting on their words, and this would cause us to prosper. The Hebrew word for prosper is *tsalach*, and it means "to push forward, advance, make progress, succeed, be prosperous."

The prophetic anointing was given so the Kingdom of God could advance, prosper and succeed. Without this help, we won't. Pretty simple. What army would choose to function without intel, recon or info from headquarters?

It is no wonder satan and his religious spirits hate this gift so much.

Tsalach, by the way, is also used in Joshua 1:8

> *This book of the law shall not depart from your mouth, but you shall meditate on it day and night, so that you may be careful to do according to all that is written in it; for then you will make your way prosperous, and then you will have success.*

As Christians, we understand the power of God's word, and certainly, the scriptures are the only infallible source of His word we have. No one I know in the prophetic world disagrees with this. All of them acknowledge that we prophesy in part and all prophecy is to be judged. But even though prophecy isn't on a par with scripture, 2 Chronicles 20:20 promises the same success from believing and acting on accurate prophetic words as it does from meditation on scripture!

Ezra 5:2 and 6:14, mentioned above, speak of the support provided and the success achieved in building the Temple through the prophesying of the prophets. The insinuation is that they would not have enjoyed success without this help.

Given this evidence, why would God hamstring the Church today by asking us to function without this wonderful gift? The answer, of course, is that He hasn't. Personally, I can't imagine trying to accomplish my assignment for Christ without the benefit of His prophetic anointing.

One often overlooked expression of the prophetic dimension, and the topic of this book, is dreaming. The concept of God speaking to us through dreams is amazing and fascinating. Think about it: "Since you will no doubt be distracted at times by your conscious mind,"

4

God says, "I'll wait until it goes to sleep and simply bypass it. You'll awaken with my strategy."

I love it!

It seems that the more strategic the times, the more Holy Spirit employs this gift and weapon. For example, at the conception and later, protection of the Christ child, dreams were prevalent. In Acts, as the early church advanced, dreams played a significant role. Little wonder, then, that in this strategic time, the number of dreams currently being given to the Church is on the increase. Whether regarding strategy to advance kingdom causes here in America or evangelizing Muslims in other nations—thousands are receiving dreams revealing Christ to them—dreams are on the uptick.

Because of this, my spirit leaped when I heard about this book by my prophetic friend, Clay Nash. More believers need to tap into this resource. Clay's dreams are profound. God has used him on numerous occasions to release important and strategic insight to me through dreams. My spirit rejoices when I see a text from Clay that begins with, "I had a dream last night." I know when I see those words that something significant is about to be shared with me. As you read this book, you'll see why.

The dreams in this collection are timely, strategic words for our nation. Don't read them only as intriguing pictures or encouraging insights, but also as key strategies for prayer and action. They are given to us, just as were the prophetic words from Haggai and Zechariah to Israel, to help us prosper and advance.

I take them very seriously. You should too!

Enjoy!

Dutch Sheets
Network Ekklesia International

Foreword by Chuck Pierce

Many people are sharing their dreams at this time. Deep within us, God is unlocking our future through the revelation He is communicating in our dreams. In the Bible, there are over 50 references for messages being sent by God through dreams and visions to both the righteous and the unrighteous alike. The Lord used dreams and visions to guide, to warn, to direct, to help—to communicate His heart. God has not stopped communicating to humanity by these means.

A dream is a release of revelation (whether natural or spiritual) that comes at a time when your body is at peace and you are settled. A dream is like a snapshot of something you are able to relate to in picture form. Ecclesiastes 5:3 tells us that a dream comes when there are many cares. They can either be a subconscious response to the circumstances of our lives, or the Holy Spirit communicating to us.

In God Dreams to Make America Great Again, Apostle Clay Nash shares an amazing collection of dreams and visions pertaining to the future of the United States of America. Like few others, he seeks the Lord for the fullest meaning of these complex communications. As you read each chapter, I declare not only will your heart be stirred to intercede for the destiny of this nation, but your own dream life will awaken with a new sense of clarity.

As Jane Hamon states in her book, Dreams and Visions, "Dreams are formed in the subconscious mind of a man or woman based on images and symbols which are unique to the individual, depending on his or her background, experience and current life circumstances. Dreams can communicate to us truth about ourselves—or others—which our conscious mind may have failed to acknowledge. Dreams can originate strictly within the natural mind or can be given as messages from God's Spirit and received

8

within the mind of man … If we compare the communication of the Spirit of the Lord through dreams to other methods of divine communication mentioned in Scripture— prophecy, a word of knowledge, etc.—the primary difference is that dreams are given first to our subconscious minds before being perceived by our conscious minds."

The easiest way to describe a vision is as if you are having a dream, but you are awake. To those experiencing a vision, it will often seem as if they have entered into a different reality because they are seeing with their spiritual eyes images of items and events that are not physically there. Others in the room may not see what is going on. That is because what is being perceived by the one or ones having the vision is a spiritual event.

Discernment is Key!

"For God may speak in one way, or in another, yet man does not perceive it. In a dream, in a vision of the night, when deep sleep falls upon men, while slumbering on their beds, Then He opens the ears of men, and seals their instruction" (Job 33:14-16).

There are three types of dreams that we find in the Bible:

1. A simple message dream. Joseph in Matthew 1-2 understood the dreams concerning Mary and Herod. There was really no need for interpretation; the dreams interpreted themselves.

2. The simple symbolic dream. Dreams can be filled with symbols, but the symbolism can be clear enough that the dreamer and others can understand it without any complicated interpretation. For instance, when Joseph had his dream in Genesis 37, he fully understood it, even though it had symbols of the sun, moon and stars. So did his brothers, to the point that they wanted to kill him.

3. The complex symbolic dream. This third type of dream needs interpretative skill from someone who has unusual ability in the gift of interpretation or someone who knows how to seek God to find revelation. We find this in the life of Joseph in prison as well as when he interprets Pharaoh's dream. In Daniel 2 and 4, we find good examples of this type of dream. In Daniel 8, we see a dream where Daniel actually had to seek divine interpretation.

Included in this book, Clay gives examples of all three of these groups of dreams. As you read, prepare to be activated with a call to see your nation great again! Get ready to dream again!

Chuck D. Pierce

Glory of Zion International, President

Global Spheres Inc., President

Introduction

I was in Denton, Texas, listening to Dutch Sheets speak, when I saw a vision of a man standing behind Dutch. He was dressed in period clothes of the 16th century, and he was holding a sign made of cloth. It bore the number 313.

I asked the Lord who he was, and the Lord said "John Knox."

I knew that John Knox was a great Scottish reformer and intercessor in the 1500s.

Later, I investigated the number 313. I found that the Strong's number for 313 was the Greek word for "born again." This exploded in my spirit, but I knew there was more.

I asked the Lord, "What else are you trying to show me?"

He replied "Day of the year."

I did a quick calculation and realized that election day was the 313rd day of the year. This was the election in which Donald Trump was running for President of the United States.

That same night, Chuck Pierce prophesied to Dutch that he was to travel to the seven places in our nation where covenant came to our nation.

- Cape Henry – destiny
- Jamestown – family and Ekklesia
- Plymouth – government, prayer, evangelism
- Boston – justice and liberty
- Philadelphia – government and mercy
- York, PA – provision and voice of the Lord
- Washington, DC – expansion and prosperity

I have learned, in 38 years of servanthood to the King of Kings, to position my spirit to be quieted before posturing myself to hear and recognize His voice. I also realize God's word is true, that "younger men see visions and older men dream dreams.

It was during this journey that my dream life began to go to another level. Today, I am convinced that God has given me stewardship of certain dreams involving our nation, our president and prominent ministers such as Dutch Sheets. To be clear, however, I don't pray for these dreams. I don't ask God for dreams. God gives me dreams and I seek Him for the interpretation.

This book is a collection of those dreams and visions pertaining to the future of the United States of America. They are mostly my dreams, a few are by others, and each is identified by the dreamer.

The figure of Dutch Sheets plays a prominent role in these dreams, as do other seasoned ministers. Because of this, I need to stress that most of these dreams are not specifically about Dutch or any other leader. Instead, the figure of Dutch represents greater things.

Dream language is largely symbolic. Because Dutch and I are close friends and work together in ministry, when God wants to show me things, Dutch (among others) is used to represent these things in my dreams.

Dutch Sheets represents a leading apostolic voice to the body of Christ. He also represents a prayer movement in America. Finally, he represents, in part, the Ekklesia, the legislative body of the church in America.

Of course, Dutch is not the only one to symbolize something. Other leaders may represent the voice of the prophetic or governmental power. The symbolism will be explained in the interpretation of the dream.

Donald Trump, who also appears frequently in these dreams, represents God's legislative government in the Nation. He is symbolic of a representative government that seeks and follows God's will for the nation.

Of course, Dutch, Trump, myself... indeed, all leaders, are mere men and women, people who carry a mantle of God's authority in heaven and on earth. And while people come and go, God's Kingdom is forever.

These dreams are about that Kingdom.

Each dream is arranged in three parts:

1. The actual dream.

2. The interpretation of the dream.

3. The decrees, declarations and prayers arising from the dream.

We know from Daniel that dream interpretation comes from the Lord.

Daniel answered before the king and said, "As for the mystery about which the king has inquired, neither wise

men, conjurers, magicians nor diviners
are able to declare it to the king."

Daniel 2:27

Indeed, there is a God in heaven, and He reveals the mysteries of what He is doing.

May these dreams inspire you, comfort you, challenge you, and most of all, call you to action. For...

The effective prayer of a righteous man
can accomplish much.

James 5:16

February 06, 2018

A Tuning Fork and Gavel

Clay Nash

I dreamed of the Turnaround gathering, a meeting which was to be held in DC at the Trump Hotel. In the meeting, there were hundreds of angels with tuning forks in their hands. Rees Howells [Rees was a Welsh intercessor in the mid-1900s, used greatly by Holy Spirit to turn the tide of WWII] and John Knox [a great Scottish reformer and intercessor in the 1500s] came in from the cloud of witnesses. Rees held a tuning fork, John a gavel. They presented these to Dutch Sheets; as they did, he smiled at his wife, Ceci, and struck them together. The angels simultaneously struck their tuning forks. As the sound permeated the people, they began to vibrate and spin and morph into an Army of Special Forces. Light came from them and filled the room.

Then a man pinned a badge on Dutch that said: U.S. MARSHALL OF THE NEW SOUND.

> *When Jesus arrived in the villages of Caesarea Philippi, he asked his disciples, "What are people saying about who the Son of Man is?"*
>
> *They replied, "Some think he is John the Baptizer, some say Elijah, some Jeremiah or one of the other prophets."*
>
> *He pressed them, "And how about you? Who do you say I am?"*
>
> *Simon Peter said, "You're the Christ, the Messiah, the Son of the living God."*
>
> *Jesus came back, "God bless you, Simon, son of Jonah! You didn't get that answer out of books or from teachers. My Father in heaven, God*

20

himself, let you in on this secret of who I really am. And now I'm going to tell you who you are, really are. You are Peter, a rock. This is the rock on which I will put together my church, a church so expansive with energy that not even the gates of hell will be able to keep it out.

"And that's not all. You will have complete and free access to God's kingdom, keys to open any and every door: no more barriers between heaven and earth, earth and heaven. A yes on earth is yes in heaven. A no on earth is no in heaven."

Matthew 16:13-19 MSG

INTERPRETATION

"hundreds of angels with tuning forks"— angels will be there to assist us in hearing the

21

sound of heaven and synchronizing to move in heaven's time.

"Rees Howells and John Knox"—we will be building on and agreeing with the prayers and reforming actions of past generations (something Dutch Sheets refers to in his book *An Appeal to Heaven* as "the synergy of the ages")

"tuning fork"—we will hear a pure and clear sound from heaven regarding America

"gavel"—the Sovereign Judge of heaven and earth is going to render His verdict as the Ekklesia legislate heaven's will into the earth.

"as the sound began permeating the people"—we will become one with/agree with heaven's words and verdicts and function as a fitly joined together body by what each joint supplies.

"they morphed into an Army of Special Forces"—just as special forces are hidden, small in number and incredibly efficient, so will we operate

"illumination came from them"—we will be filled with and release revelation and glory

"U.S. Marshall of the new sound"—we will function as Christ's Ekklesia, the representatives of His kingdom government on earth; as such, we will expose the enemies of God, disrupt their plans, enforce heaven's rule, and reform America.

> *Truly, truly, I say to you, he who believes in Me, the works that I do, he will do also; and greater works than these he will do; because I go to the Father.*

John 14:12

The passage speaks of revelation; the authority of Christ; Christ's Ekklesia—the representatives of His Kingdom government on earth; binding and loosing; and releasing Heaven's judgments against the powers of hell.

Psalms 149 tells us all the saints are honored with the potential of participating in this activity. Could it be that God is about to shift the praying earth into a new dimension of all this? I believe so. The finest days of the Church are not behind us; they are ahead. Let's write history together!

DECREES

We declare the release of the synergy of the intercessors and reformers from the cloud of witnesses.

We declare the release of a clear sound of worship, intercession, and decrees.

We agree in faith decreeing that the Supreme Judge of all the universe is releasing rulings and that we will hear, receive, and we will respond in agreement with His decrees.

Pray and decree that all assembled to see this nation's turnaround will become one, moving together in oneness of faith and obedience.

We Declare that a new sound of justice is being released into and through the body of Christ facilitating our Nation's turnaround.

We Decree that the Ekklesia is truly becoming one with God's will.

We pray for the release of the sound through which we become one. We specifically pray for this sound to be released through the worship, declarations, decrees, and preaching.

Decree that pure revelation and spiritual understanding will come to us and be released from us.

Decree that the Church and the Worldwide Prayer Movements are going to new expressions of Kingly anointing and authority, in order to function as His Ekklesia.

2019

POTUS Request

Clay Nash

I dreamed that Dutch Sheets and a small group of us were invited to see President Trump in the Oval Office. Upon arrival, after some small talk, Trump, very much in humility, began to thank Dutch for his leadership and the Appeal to Heaven prayer movement. Trump then presented Dutch with an Appeal to Heaven flag that he had signed.

Trump then requested that Dutch organize a high level, strategic prayer task force. He told Dutch he would be releasing directly to him significant issues for prayer. He also said that he had received this prophetic instruction from a very trusted voice—his wife, Melania.

Dutch presented Trump with a white stone and read to him from Revelation:

To him who overcomes, to him I will give some of the hidden manna, and I will give him a white stone, and a new name written on the stone which no one knows but he who receives it.

Revelation 2:17

Trump then quoted to you:

There came a man sent from God, whose name was John.

John 1:6

Trump then asked if he could pray for all of us. In his prayer, he said, "Lord, let this man and these leaders convene a holy convocation that I might finish my eight years well, and the ancient markers of our founding fathers be restored."

He then presented to Dutch a pager and said, "When you see the number 2222, always answer your cell phone even though it will have no caller ID."

28

He who has an ear, let him hear what the Spirit says to the churches. To him who overcomes, to him I will give some of the hidden manna, and I will give him a white stone, and a new name written on the stone which no one knows but he who receives it.

Revelation 2:17

INTERPRETATION

In this dream, we see the highest office of authority in our nation calling upon the highest authority of the church—the Ekklesia and the praying—being honored by President Donald "John the Beloved" Trump.

President Trump presenting to the Ekklesia an *Appeal to Heaven* flag with his signature represents the endorsement of national governmental authority to the Ekklesia and praying church.

The request to form a high-level strategic prayer task force displays President Trump's understanding that he needs God's intervention to fulfill his assignment.

His informing Dutch that he would communicate significant issues directly to him for is Dutch representing the Ekklesia and praying church.

The trusted prophetic voice from his wife is a sign of the trust of the power of agreement with those in spiritual authority.

The new name on a white stone speaks of him coming into the fulfillment of his relationship with God and becoming John the Beloved.

The man sent from, is reference that he understands he was chosen by God as a Cyrus to our nation.

The Holy Convocation refers to the Appeal to Heaven Reset 2020 being held in Middletown, Ohio on October 8-10.

The number 2222 refers to Isaiah 22:22 and keys to lock and unlock. It is also Dutch Sheet's life scripture.

> *Then I will set the key of the house of*
> *David on his shoulder,*
> *When he opens no one will shut,*
> *When he shuts no one will open.*

DECREES

We decree that as the Ekklesia, the praying church, and President Donald *John the Beloved* Trump partner together, Heaven's will shall be done for our nation and the November 2020 election.

We declared that every assembly for prayer that has taken place and will take place will become a *Kairos* time for the November Election.

31

We declare the Keys of David will be used to *lock* evil agendas and *unlock* Heaven's strategy for President Trump's re-election and four more years of righteous turnaround.

We declare that answers from Heaven will be given to everyone praying and interceding on behalf of God's will for our Nation.

February 6, 2018

America Shall Be Saved

Gina Gholston (of Clarksville TN)

I dreamed that I, two friends (fellow intercessors) and my mom and dad, were walking down Pennsylvania Avenue in Washington, D.C. I knew the Turnaround Conference at the Trump Hotel was just ending at that very moment. I turned and saw a courier coming out of the doors of the building as the conference was ending.

This was an angel. He was carrying a large scroll and to the U.S. Capitol Building. We followed him as he entered the building. We went into the House Chambers.

It was the scene of the State of the Union address given by President Trump a few nights ago. All the lawmakers were there in their seats and there were many people in the gallery. It was packed.

The courier angel with the scroll was standing at the double doors that the President had entered through, and the angel announced, "All Rise!"

And just as had happened at the previous State of the Union Address, some people stood while others disrespectfully stayed seated.

The angel then opened the scroll and proclaimed: "The verdict has been determined: AMERICA SHALL BE SAVED!"

Immediately a glory cloud of God came from behind the angel and filled the room. Those who had stood at Trump's entrance were now kneeling, wailing, broken by God's presence. Some (maybe two or three) who had remained seated were now on their knees, screaming: "I'm sorry! I'm SO SORRY!!!" Others remained seated. Judgement was being administered and God's ruling authority was established! It was transformation and reformation being established for America's new reality:

America shall be saved!

INTERPRETATION

There is a connection between those who have gone before us and those who have taken their place. The prayer movement in our nation is the joining of the generations and the uniting of the Ekklesia.

Heaven is responding! God has heard our cries for this nation and has sent an announcement from heaven declaring His verdict to our petition: "America shall be saved!"

The Courier angel received the verdict and was sent to deliver that message to the halls of Congress. This move of God will be a national move affecting government and the nation as a whole. It is time to revive and improve the spiritual landscape of the nation.

We have entered a time of elevated warfare for the destiny of our nation, and God was showing us through this dream, *ahead of time,* that regardless of what transpires in the days ahead, the outcome has been determined:

America shall be saved!

This truth must be held in the minds of the praying church. This is God's will and we must press into it! This is His plan and we set our expectations for it to be even as He has spoken.

DECREES

Father, You gave our founding fathers the wisdom and ability to bring this nation into alignment with Your eternal intentions for the development of a land of religious freedom and a voice of liberty that would declare Your goodness throughout the world. Thank you for raising up this great nation. Thank you for those who took their place in their time to move this nation on the path of Your purposes and intentions.

We know that satan would love to shift this nation from its original path and lead it into darkness. He has sent forth those who seek to carry out his plans and intentions, but You have a remnant who refused to abandon Your intentions. You have heard the cries of the generations and You have responded with Your verdict:"

We as Your legislative body, Your Ekklesia, take that verdict and declare with the backing of Your authority, "Be it so!"

We rise with an unquenchable resolve to move with You and for You to see Your will in our nation!

We declare the downfall and annihilation of every scheme of hell that has been sent to change laws and times to throw this nation off its course and destiny. Those snares are broken!

Those plots and schemes meet with a defeated end! Hell will not prevail against America!

We stand with this truth: "America shall be saved," and we speak it into our upcoming elections.

Those who You have ordained to occupy the seats of government in this land will occupy those seats, and they will govern by the influence of Holy Spirit as He leads this nation forward.

We declare that the foundations of our Godly heritage will remain firm and unshaken. Your Glory, O, God, will blanket this nation, catapulting us into an awareness of the reality of You and Your Christ!

This is the turning point! Regardless of the intentions of the radical leftist agenda to change the course of America, we stand up in this moment and join with the host of heaven to declare Your verdict! Your verdict stands! Your verdict remains as our undeniable truth.

America shall be saved!

In Jesus' name, amen!

April 7, 2020

President Trump and the Wooden Crate

Gina Gholston (of Clarksville TN)

I dreamed President Donald J. Trump was walking on the bank of a small river. At first, it seemed he was pacing back and forth, but then I realized he was actually looking for something. He said, "I was told something had been left for me here, and I came to find it. I thought I could find it here, but I'm not seeing it."

He continued to search, but finding nothing, he turned to walk away.

Just as he turned, there was a wooden crate bobbing up in the water, about three feet by two feet by one foot. I saw through the water several people lying on the bottom of the river. They had been holding that box but they lost their

41

grip on it, and it rushed to the surface with a splash. President Trump reached pulled it to the bank, took a knife from his pocket and opened the crate.

Inside, he found an old Bible, an Appeal to Heaven flag, and communion elements (a cup of wine and some bread). He draped the Appeal to Heaven flag over his shoulders, then knelt with the old Bible on his left forearm and the bread and wine in his left and right hands. With tears flowing from his eyes, he prayed. Looking down at the Bible and communion elements with admiration, he said, "This is it! This is what I came to find!"

A huge slingshot suddenly appeared and Trump positioned himself in it. A hand pulled him back and launched him out from that place. The items in the crate were carried with him.

Just as he was launched, the people in the river came out and tried to grab Trump but it was too late. He was already airborne and they couldn't touch him.

He made a perfect upright landing on a stage in front of the Capitol Building in Washington, D.C. It was Inauguration Day and he was giving an inaugural address but it wasn't a normal speech. He put the Appeal to Heaven flag around his shoulders and held that old Bible in his hands. I realized this was the Bible that he had been sworn in with at his last Inauguration ceremony. I believe it belonged to his mother who had connections to the great Welsh Revival.

President Trump was still crying, and he said, "God is taking us back, and He's giving us a new start. Now we are rightly focused. We're getting back on track."

He led the nation in a prayer of sincere repentance, then he led the nation in communion with the elements in his hands.

INTERPRETATION

This dream speaks of current and future events in America.

There is an evil attempt to keep what is true, righteous, and holy from being brought to the surface of awareness in this nation, but we are coming to the moment when it won't be withheld any longer. It may seem a last-minute move, but what God has reserved and preserved for this moment in time is going to make its presence known with a splash. Truth will be found and revealed. Eyes will be opened to the revelation of Jesus. Hearts will be opened to receive His love and truth, and there will be an awakening to God in our President and our nation.

President Trump's retrieval of the revealed wooden crate and the use of his knife to open it signifies a deep, spiritual awakening coming to President Donald John Trump. He is going to find what he has been searching for, which is a deeper awareness of God and the revelation of Jesus Christ. When he found the flag, the Bible and the communion elements, his eyes were opened, his heart was touched and he was humbled before the Lord. This awakened a realization in him: "This is what I came to find!"

This is the answer for our nation, and he put on that prayer mantle (the Appeal to Heaven flag), and embraced Christ (the communion elements) and Truth (the old Bible). From this personal transformation, he was launched into the next part of his destiny. He was re-positioned, and the things that he had gathered from that personal encounter gave him proper perspective of how to lead the nation—first and foremost, back to God.

The attempt to keep Trump from launching from the slingshot reveals the current massive, desperate effort to take Trump out of his position and to deny him the ability to be re-positioned. It is an all-out attempt to firmly and finally get this nation turned away from God and His original plans and intentions for this land. But it's too late! The hand of God is ready to launch Donald Trump into position to continue to lead this nation, but this time it will be different. This is America's turnaround moment!

America is set for an awakening to an awareness of God. The Bible President Trump carried has a connection to the great revival in the nation of Wales. This shows that America will be revived back to her godly roots and destiny. Also, the President's leading the nation in repentance and communion speaks of redemption and restoration. Finally, his sincere declaration over the nation speaks strongly of an unfolding national awakening to God

God is taking us back, and He's giving us a new start. Now we are rightly focused. We're getting back on track. God is not finished with America!

DECREES

Father, you ordained from the foundation of the world, the founding of these United States of America. Known of you from the beginning of time were your plans and intentions for this nation. We see your hand at work throughout the pages of our history. You have guided us by your divine Providence and wisdom. Now, we stand at the moment that you have determined to be the "hinge of history," and we see that the godly future of our nation is being weighed in the balance. Evil is attempting to withhold the reality of you and your truth from the hearts of the people of this land. But we, as your Ekklesia, release our voices in agreement with you, and we say, "Let your Kingdom come! Let your will be done" in America! Our Godly heritage and purpose as a nation will not be lost nor forsaken. We declare: "God arises and every enemy scatters!"

We decree that evil is losing its grip. The revelation of Jesus Christ and your Word is making a comeback! Awakening to an awareness of God is now rising to the surface and will be released in an unstoppable move of power and demonstration of the Spirit of God that will turn the focus back to God and get us back on track with His original plans and intentions for us and for the existence of our nation!

Father, against all odds, you have raised up and positioned Donald Trump as President of the United States of America. You positioned him to be a leader who stands as a defender of the nation of Israel, of the unborn, of your church and your righteous laws. Even in the heat of massive pressure and resistance, he has stood—by your divine strength—to accomplish many of the purposes for which you have positioned him. You positioned him, and he will remain in that position until you say otherwise. We ask that you continue to strengthen him and to guide him by your Spirit. Protect him and his family from any and all attempts that are made to harm them. Protect him from any and all attempts that are made in an effort to remove him from the destiny you have chosen for his life. May he have a personal encounter with you that will forever transform his life and deepen his relationship with you. May he humble himself to walk with you. May your Word be embedded in his heart, establishing him on the foundation of your unchanging Truth! And as the President of these United States of America, may his voice be released as a trumpet that calls this nation back to you!

Father, you know the plans you have woven over this nation. You see and know every part that must be in place in order for your plans to be implemented. We agree with you for those plans to prevail. We are confident that the good work you have begun in this nation, you will carry it through to the completion that you have intended. No evil or evil intentions will succeed in stopping what you have purposed for America. You are drawing the hearts of the people back to yourself, and you are giving us a new start. Now we are rightly focused, and we're getting back on track…and this train is bound for Glory—the unveiling of the unavoidable knowledge and awareness of your manifested presence covering America and the world as the waters cover the sea!

April 26, 2020

Stand In The River

Clay Nash

I dreamed that the Body of Christ was standing at the Jordan River. Dutch Sheets was there and he told us that today was April 30th. Then he said that we must step into the water and stand steadfastly until the old flow dries up and the new flow comes. He said the flow was drying up 11 miles upstream at the City of Adam, and that once it completely dried up, we would move into our promise of the land being healed.

INTERPRETATION

This dream points to the land being healed due to repentance and obedient actions of the people.

This dream interpretation draws on two parallels.

The first is from Joshua 3 when Joshua led Israel across the Jordan river. As long as the priests stood in the middle of the river, the water flow was halted at the City of Adam 11 miles upstream and the people could cross on dry ground.

The second is the dream had by Will Ford's seven-year-old son who dreamed that the Corona virus would dissipate on 30 April. He had the same dream seven times with little deviation.

I researched April 30th and found that it is the 121 day of the year. The Strong's number in Hebrew for 121 is *aw-dawm'* or Adam. In Joshua 3, the flow of water stopped 11 miles upstream at the City of Adam.

In Joshua 3, the priests had to stand in the water until 11 miles of the old flow dried up. So it is today. When we see the old flow drying up and the new flow coming, we can step into the promise of the land being healed.

The new flow is bringing the promise of 2 Chronicles 7:13-14.

If I [God] shut up the heavens...and My people who are called by My name humble themselves and pray and seek My face and turn from their wicked ways, then I will hear from heaven, will forgive their sin and will heal their land.

Note, however, the conditional phrase *"If... my people..."*

DECREES

We decree and declare that our obedience of a steadfast stand of faith is bringing about the Kingdom result of the old flow across our nation drying up and a new flow—a tsunami of God's glory—is coming.

We declare that as a result of our land being healed, we will move forward in our inheritances and see God's original intent, restored along with the ancient boundaries and markers of our fathers.

We decree that the new flow of God's Spirit will facilitate our entrance and completion of God's promise to us of our land being healed.

Cane Ridge

Clay Nash

I dreamed that Dutch took a team to Cane Ridge, Kentucky, to decree into the land to bring forth the power of Pentecost that was once released there.

We arrived in several vans and found a large crowd there. Ray Hughes was preaching to the crowd. When he saw Dutch, he called him up to preach.

Ray and Dutch began to tag-preach and the preaching went through the night. When the sun came up the next morning, there people surrounding the ridge as far as the eye could see. The power of the Spirit was falling and people were being slain in the Spirit and speaking in tongues.

Ray and Dutch continued preaching for three days and nights. Then they started a fire tunnel for people to go forth and release what had been stirred up in them. The fire tunnel took 24 hours to complete and finished at midnight.

Ray and Dutch rested around a fire, and in the morning, there were thousands more new people there. A man approach Ray and Dutch and said he was buying each of them a new motorhome to rest in because they could not leave yet.

The dream recycled over and over until I saw a headline from USA Today which said:

After 44 Days and Nights of
Preaching at Cane Ridge, Kentucky,
America Burns with Revival.

The Pockets of a Fiery Awakening
Burning Across the Nation Are
Spreading, Bringing Public Life to a
Standstill

INTERPRETATION

Cane Ridge, Kentucky, is the location of the largest and most famous camp meeting of the Second Great Awakening. It was a continuation of the outpouring that began at the Red River Meeting House in 1800.

From August 6 to 13, 1801, an estimated 20,000 – 30,000 people (roughly 10% of the population of Kentucky) attended for all or part of the meeting.

Years later, people who had experienced a life-changing transformation as a result of God's presence, requested that when they die, that they would be buried there. This resulted in people being buried six to eight people deep. No matter. The people wanted to return to the place where their lives began anew.

In the dream, I knew that this modern-day gathering was not pre-arranged. Dutch did not know Ray was going to be there; Ray did not know Dutch was going to be there. The significance of both of them there at the same time is important to the interpretation.

Ray Hughes is from Kentucky, so he's married to the land there. He represents the history of the land of Kentucky and the history of Cane Ridge. He and Dutch together represent the Apostolic (Dutch) and the Prophetic (Ray) for sending people out from the history of the Second Great Awakening to start the Third Great Awakening.

The fire tunnel represents hands being laid on people for anointing and authority to stir up the fire—the Spirit of God—and being sent forth from apostles and prophets to do the works of ministry they are called to. This will work in bringing about the Third Great Awakening in our nation.

DECREES

We declare that the hunger of people is increasing for the outpouring of God's Spirit and power.

We declare that apostles and prophets are working together to establish God's foundation and equip and align God's people in their purpose and destiny.

We decree that the pause that will result from outbreaks of the stirring of anointing will result in God's Army being joined by angel armies to accomplish Kingdom breakthroughs.

March 26, 2020

Valley Forge

Clay Nash

This involves two dreams and some backstory.

DREAM I

I dreamed that Dutch Sheets was on a walking trail at Valley Forge, Pennsylvania—the historical encampment of George Washington's Continental Army—and the Angel who spoke mercy six times to Dutch and Tim Sheets while they were in Washington, D.C. (explained in the interpretation) appeared to him on the trail.

The angel presented Dutch with 12 stones and said they came from the Delaware River. He told Dutch that as he walked, he would come upon an unusual tree distinguished by its bent shape.

Dutch was to place the 12 stones under the bent part of the tree as a memorial attesting to the fact that angels have been released and the spiritual war for the soul of our nation is beginning to turn.

In the dream, I was positioned like a guard watching Dutch's back through intercession. I had no weapon but I was positioned on a hill and could see his actions clearly at all times.

The tree where he placed the 12 stones was bent over near the base. After Dutch placed the stones, he turned to leave. As he walked along the trail, a man stepped from behind a tree. It startled me because I had not seen him. He was dressed in clothes of a much earlier era.

He introduced himself to Dutch as William Penn. He said that because Dutch was a man who kept his word, even when it cost him, God was releasing to him the stewardship ability of

Elijah, which is to speak words and have God honor those words out of the covenant relationship between Dutch and God.

Then the man disappeared and Dutch walked out of the trail.

BACKSTORY

A few years ago, Dutch Sheets was in Washington, D.C. with his brother Tim Sheets and also Ken Malone. They were at the White House pray, standing apart from the crowd that is normally in front of the White House. As they were praying, a man walked toward them saying "mercy, mercy, mercy, mercy, mercy, mercy."

As strange as this was, the man kept walking right past the three. They tried to call him back but he wouldn't look at them. He headed straight into the crowd and disappeared.

They knew he was an angel.

Coinciding with this experience, there is a minister out of St. Louis who recently dreamed of a rain of coins—each bearing the word "mercy."

Dutch understood this to mean that the new currency for America is mercy.

DREAM II

I dreamed that Dutch Sheets texted me and said, "Clear your schedule and make plans to meet me in Valley Forge. Bill Olsen had a dream that there were angels on reserve there that must be called into active duty. We must go as one to do so."

Bill Olson is a spiritual son to Dutch. He has a military background. He presented the original Appeal To Heaven flag that brought Dutch into revelation about its history to our Nation.

INTERPRETATION

I shared both dreams with Dutch—the dream of him doing an assignment at Valley Forge and the dream of him telling me to clear my schedule.

Sometime later, Bill Olsen came to visit Dutch. He did not know about the dreams I had concerning him or Dutch or Valley Forge. During his visit, he told Dutch, "I've been studying on Valley Forge, and you have to do an assignment there."

He then gave Dutch a book on Valley Forge. This confirmed to Dutch that he needed to do the assignment.

A member of Dutch's team went to William Penn Park, which is on the Delaware River, collected 12 river stones and gave them to Dutch, who took them to Valley Forge, Virginia.

William Penn park, and the presence of
William Penn in my dream, are significant
because William Penn—the founder of
Pennsylvania—was the only man who kept
every treaty he made with the American
Indians. In one instance, he even paid twice for
a piece of land after a dispute arose, just to keep
the peace.

Now, when Dutch got there, Valley Forge
was closed due to the Covid virus, but Dutch
explained to a park ranger that he was there on
a prayer assignment. The ranger said, "As long
as you are going to be walking and praying, I'll
let you in there."

Dutch followed a walking trail. During his
walk, he was connected by phone with several
intercessors who were actively praying. He
discovered a peculiar tree right beside George
Washington's quarters, and received a strong
witness that this was the tree. Dutch also felt the
presence of the angel that I'd seen in the dream,

the same angel that had repeated "mercy" six times to him in Washington, D.C.

So, he placed the stones there.

The 12 stones are a memorial to the angel army being released into our nation. Twelve is the number of God's government.

Valley Forget is where the Revolutionary Army was forged into a fighting force. The conditions there were brutal, yet it unified the army, which was vital to its success.

DECREES

We declare and decree that the newly released angel army is on active duty and ready to co-labor with God's army of people.

We declare that these angels are being released from that historical location of Valley Forge will help secure breakthrough as God is forging a new level of warfare in and thru His Ekklesia.

Let Heaven's will be done here on earth!

We declare that just as our Nation came from a great battle at Valley Forge, so we are now battling forth into a great victory of our nation's Christian heritage.

April 23, 2020

Model, Tennessee

Clay Nash

I dreamed that Dutch Sheets summoned a team of people to meet him in Model, Tennessee. I was among them.

When we arrived, we found ourselves at a huge stone furnace for melting iron. It was fired up and full of molten iron. Dutch instructed us to help him in forming and engraving iron plaques. The plaques were poured and while still hot, we engraved them with these words:

Despite the hardships presently, the United States is the birthplace of the Ekklesia Army being forged for the New Era. By June 2020, the Ekklesia Army will emerge with a rejuvenated spirit and a confidence to function as a well-trained fighting force.

Dutch embossed each plague on the back with President Trump's signature. Dutch told us that the President had given him Power of Attorney to sign his name.

Dutch then instructed us to transport these plaques while still hot, to the Red River Meeting House (in Kentucky) to be submerged in the water there to cool and molt before they were distributed to the nation.

Dutch then instructed that the distribution was to begin at Valley Forge, Pennsylvania, and move out to the Nation from there.

INTERPRETATION

The town of Model, Tenn. Died out in the early 1900s. Today, there is only a huge stone furnace for melting iron exist. (I did not know of Model this before the dream.)

The interpretation rests on two points.

1. Pentecost weekend was 28-31 May, 2020. In the days following Pentecost, many Christians said something shifted in the spirit. They felt a lightness in the spirit, a refreshing, that the glory of God was being released in a greater way.

2. In this dream, Dutch represents President Donald Trump giving the Ekklesia (the legislative arm of Body of Christ) Power of Attorney—the highest power in the land—to sign his signature.

This is symbolic of the two authorities in the land—the natural and the spiritual—coming together.

The plaques being carried to the Red River Meeting House is important because historically, government met there and churches met there. This, again, represents the union of natural and spiritual.

Carrying plates there to cool by immersing them in the river speaks to the Second Great

Awakening as a foundation for the present movement of awakening—the synergy of the ages. Where we tap into the prayers, build, gives us synergy release. We are building on prayers of people from hundreds of years ago.

When David heard of Goliath intimidating the army of Israel, he asked: "Is there not a cause?" Meaning: *Is there not a history?* David was rallying his historical roots. He was of the tribe of Judea, and now he was at the forefront to repel the attack of the enemy of God's people in the form of Goliath. He represented the Nation of Israel. David was saying: "This land is ours. You are not taking it away from us."

Today, we are tapping into the history of the Red Rock Meeting House. This is a timely message because so many people are weary; they have been wearied by the spiritual battle.

The message of this dream is to harken back to our roots to know where we are headed in God.

DECREES

We decree and declare that the soul of our Nation will not be stolen.

We declare, God, that we have entered your time of rejuvenation of the spirits and physical strength of your remnant.

God, let our minds be clear and may we have complete spiritual understanding of your Kingdom business that lies ahead.

May the apostles and prophets of our nation bring us into alignment to function as your well-trained fighting force.

8 April 2020

Recalibrate, Reset, Reconstitute

Clay Nash

It was the morning of Passover, and I dreamed that Dutch Sheets sounded a clarion call for the Ekklesia to gather at all the city gates. In the meeting, there were hundreds of seasoned fathers and mothers of the faith. Jim Hodges (who is Dutch's spiritual father) stood on a platform with Dutch, along with other men and women who carried true authority and had brought forth significant influence.

Dutch began to speak on the original intent of our nation. He spoke from history, past moves of God and current trends. He stated that during this Covid virus shutdown, God was recalibrating our hearts to Him, and that once the recalibrating was complete, a reset would take place.

He admonished those gathered together that there must be a fresh baptism of consecration, that it was time for the mothers and fathers of the Ekklesia to release the Spirit of Adoption upon sons and daughters, and that we were to baptize them, washing them with the water of the word as they were baptized.

Jim Hodges then addressed us, saying that this obedience would release a fresh inheritance to those who had been held for such a time as this. Jim Hodges then baptized Dutch.

The thing that stood out in the dream is that Jim baptized Dutch forward. As he did so, Jim spoke over Dutch, saying "This is my son, in whom I am well pleased."

Jim then instructed the assembly to go and do likewise. He shouted over and over: "Pharaoh let my people go." He continued shouting until the assembly joined in with him.

Jim then declared that God would reconstitute our nation as we followed the cloud by day (the apostles) and fire by night (the prophets).

Then I saw the front cover of Time magazine. It said:

Millions Baptized into Their Inheritances.
The Spirit of Adoption Is Upon America.

As I awoke, I heard the Spirit of the Lord say: "My day is at hand."

I wept.

INTERPRETATION

City gates represent a place of governmental and spiritual authority. In ancient times, when the Ekklesia was ready to legislate God's will, they'd meet at the city gates. They would decree God's will and town criers would walk through the city telling them what God said.

Also, when a young son showed sufficient maturity, his father would take him to the city gates and call the Ekklesia to assemble, saying "This is my son in whom I am well pleased."

At this moment, he would adopt his own son. As part of the process, he would also water baptize him forward and give him his inheritance. Note that nobody had to die for an inheritance to be given. The inheritance was given to help the son fulfill God's mandate for him, while his father was still alive.

This parallels Jesus' baptism in the Jordan River.

Dutch represents a national voice of prayer and legislative decree, hence his call to assemble the mature leaders (spiritual generals) of Body of Christ.

Dutch is speaking with an Apostolic voice to the Ekklesia. His instructions out of past and current moves of God, trends and history refer to this principle: *To possess your future, you have to understand your past.*

Jim Hodges is Dutch's spiritual father. He represents spiritual fatherhood, older and seasoned, to the mature leadership of the Ekklesia.

Of the three words: recalibrate, reset and reconstitute, they describe what is happening during this Covid 19 pause. The goal is for the apostolic and the prophetic to work together to recalibrate our nation. The Apostles send forth the people based on the vision of the prophets who are able to look through the darkness to see what God is doing.

Therefore repent and return, so that your sins may be wiped away, in order that times of refreshing may come from the presence of the Lord; and that He may send Jesus, the Christ appointed for you, whom heaven must receive until the period of restoration of all things about which God spoke by the mouth of His holy prophets from ancient time.

Acts 3:19-21

In the phrases: *repent, times of refreshing, restore,* we see another process: the *reconstitution* of all things. In that process, water is added to a dried substance to reconstitute to original form. This speaks of the outpouring of Holy Spirit (symbolized as water in Bible) to reconstitute the United States into its original form—a godly nation—as this third great awakening sweeps across the globe.

When Jim cried in the dream: "Pharaoh, let my people go!" it was obviously harkening to when Israel escaped Egypt so they could serve God. Jim's words are symbolic of the charge to religious institutions that have crippled the

80

body of Christ, to free the nation to serve God. It was a fatherly declaration of releasing the people of the nation to serve God as intended.

The words of Jim Hodges to Dutch (who symbolizes the Ekklesia) saying "This is my son in whom I am well pleased," refers to many things:

A coming release of inheritance from mature mothers and fathers to the sons and daughter of the Body of Christ.

A Spirit of Adoption, enabling people to tap into who God called them to be.

The power of agreement through water baptism is propelling us *forward* into our inheritance, which is to enable God's original intent for our lives.

Our inheritance is to be set on the road to be who God called us to be.

The Ekklesia has matured to the point where God can walk them into the Third Great

Awakening. They can receive their inheritance to accomplish it.

In the midst of recalibration and resetting, there is a revealing of hearts.

DECREES

We decree that the recalibrating of the body of Christ is bring about a fitly joining together to become more effective.

We declare that as the recalibrating is completed, a reset will bring about the result of accomplishing more with less effort.

We declare there is a rising hunger from the body of Christ to pray, intercede, declare and decree Heaven's will into our Nation, our Government, His churches, our families and our spheres of authority and influence.

We decree that the present disruptive culture will respond to Heaven's sounds and will.

We declare the answers from Heaven will be the strategy to reconstitute this Nation as the times of refreshing sweep from shore to shore.

We declare that the outpouring of Holy Spirit upon the Body of Christ in our Nation will be a Heaven's rain to reconstitute God's original intent in America.

29 April, 2020

Clay Nash

The Miracle Womb

In this dream, Chuck and Dutch were in a room called "the miracle womb." There were many others there, and everyone was dressed in medical scrubs. There was great expectancy in the air. The inside of the room was a miraculous environment. From this "miracle womb," many birthing's were taking place. As the womb birthed forth miracles, those in scrubs delivered the miracles to angels, who moved at the speed of light to deliver them to those who needed them.

The miracle womb was constantly birthing the miraculous. There were restored body parts, healings, releases of apostolic anointing for people into their original intent and ministry. There was also the birthing of finances, property and resources for ministries to reconstitute the Nation.

Chuck would speak to the womb and decree what was to come forth through birth, and Dutch would speak words of Spiritual understanding over each miracle birth. This was happening with such intensity that the people in the scrubs had to be changed out in shifts to rest.

INTERPRETATION

This dream is centered around the large miracle room that Chuck Pearce and Dutch Sheets are seeking to complete at Chuck's headquarters: Glory of Zion International, a 380,000 ft^2 ministry complex in Corinth, Texas.

Chuck is an international prophet know for the accuracy of his prophetic words. He predicted the Covid 19 virus a year before it happened.

His building includes a sanctuary to seat 1500, but he fills it every time there is a meeting. So, he has been working on a sanctuary to seat 5,000. He calls it "the miracle womb"—because it's being built miracle by miracle, and he expects that miracles will be birthed there when the building is complete.

This dream, therefore, is about the apostolic and the prophetic coming together to produce a womb (or matrix) that will produce miracles. Chuck decrees for the miracles to come forth (prophet), and Dutch speaks understanding for what is birthed to accomplish its purpose (apostle).

The presence of people in scrubs who were handing off the miracles to the angels is symbolic of the fact that people have to do their part tending to the miracles.

This is the picture of apostle and prophet and people working together with the supernatural (angels).

So then you are no longer strangers and aliens, but you are fellow citizens with the saints, and are of God's household, having been built on the foundation of the apostles and prophets, Christ Jesus Himself being the corner stone,

Ephesians 2:19-20

DECREES

We decree from your Word, God, that Ephesian's 2:20 is being fulfilled in this dream: "having been built on the foundation of the apostles and prophets, Christ Jesus Himself being the corner stone."

We declare that as Chuck and Dutch work together as Apostle and Prophet, we will see this nation become a womb of the miraculous.

We declare that as God's people work passionately from the foundation of the apostles and prophets, we will see Angel

Armies released to assist in seeing miracles take place.

We declare the movement of signs and wonders in ever increasing numbers.

We decree that Isaiah 8:18 is being fulfilled: "Behold, I and the children whom the Lord has given me are for signs and wonders in Israel from the Lord of hosts, who dwells on Mount Zion."

We declare that as the prophetic brings forth revelation, the apostolic will present clear and focused spiritual understanding.

We declare that even as those dressed in scrubs representing the "works of the ministry" needed to work together by changing out our responsibilities, we declare a fitly joining together by what each joint will supply.

We declare this womb of the miraculous will bring forth signs and wonders to cause hearts of those not surrendered to God and not fully surrendered to God to be yielded completely, causing the Third Great Awakening to grow, expand and bring about transformation across the United States of America and the world.

We declare apostles, prophets, evangelists, shepherds and teachers working together maturing, equipping and aligning the saints for greater works

> *Truly, truly, I say to you, he who believes in Me, the works that I do, he will do also; and greater works than these he will do; because I go to the Father.*
>
> John 14:12

The OK Corral

Clay Nash

I dreamed of the famous *Shootout at the OK Corral*. The dream's setting looked like Tombstone, Arizona, but it also looked like Washington, D.C. In it, President Trump was Wyatt Earp, Dutch was Doc Holiday, and there were others. (The only ones I recognized were Ted Cruz and Tom Cotton.)

It was right before the gun battle.

President Trump met with Dutch and the others at the White House and said that it was time to start cleaning up the nation. Dutch and the rest crossed the street from the White House to meet the evil ones. There was a battle in an alleyway.

The only causality was one of the evil ones. Then one of Trump's team was eliminated.

That's when Trump said, "It is time to go after them all."

Many of the evil ones were found, caught, jailed, and some were eliminated. Finally, the leader of the evil ones sent word to Trump saying he wanted to meet with Trump alone. The leader looked like a younger Mueller.

The morning Trump was to meet the leader for the showdown, Trump entered Dutch's room where he was resting. Dutch told Trump that the constant battle had made him weary. Trump told Dutch to rest and not worry; he could handle the leader of the evil ones.

In the dream, it seemed unlikely that Dutch would allow Trump to go without him.

Trump left to meet the leader of the evil ones in the designated place, and Ted Cruz and Tom Cotton went with him. As Trump neared the rendezvous, he told Ted and Tom to stay back and that he would meet the leader alone.

That's when the sound of battle rang out.

Trump ran to the location of the battle only to find Dutch standing over the leader. He had been eliminated. Trump said, "Dutch, you were weary. You should have stayed and rested. But how did you know to get to this location so quickly?"

Dutch said, "My brother, Tim, and I have been here many times with our weapons. I only wanted to make you think I was weary."

Trump smiled and said, "It's better that your weapon took this one out now. We can get the rest."

Then I saw the Atlanta Journal-Constitution headline:

The Deep State Are Finally Buried
Deep Under Their Crime.
Trump's Re-Election A Sure Thing
Now.

I feel the place that Dutch took out the leader of the evil ones was Middletown, Ohio.

INTERPRETATION

Dutch is going to hold an Appeal to Heaven for the Nation at his brother, Tim's church in Middletown, Ohio, in October. The focus will be on the election.

When Trump says, "It's better that your weapon took this one out now. We can get the rest," this refers to prayer in the spirit and the decrees of the Ekklesia for the evil ones to be pushed back defeated and Trump reelected.

Dutch is originally from Ohio. He has had many Appeal to Heaven meetings throughout the country. He says the strongest were always in Middletown, Ohio.

This dream speaks to the focus of the upcoming meeting on October 8th through 10th, 2020, and gives confirmation that God is in it.

DECREES

Father, we decree that you draw to Middletown, Ohio, the praying, decreeing church.

We declare the weapons of warfare, intercession and legislative decrees will be used to battle and eliminated the opposers of your destiny for our great nation and your Cyrus— Donald "John the Beloved" Trump.

We declare you have a strategy to eliminate those of an antichrist spirit that despise the anointing on President Trump.

We declare as one puts a thousand to flight and two ten thousand.

We declare that those assembled in Middletown will be postured to bring breakthrough to our nation's next vital election.

May 27, 2020

Eve of Pentecost

Dwain Miller (of Little Rock, Arkansas)

For the third time in as many days, I dreamed that Dutch Sheets stood before President Trump on the White House lawn. Standing behind Dutch was the Ekklesia. I recognized most of them, but there were at least a thousand people I could see and more on the horizon.

President Trump looked like a deflated balloon figure almost out of helium, bent over and tired. Dutch began to prophesy to him that only the Holy Spirit could revive and refill him. The Ekklesia began to pray, prophesy and decree into his administration and re-election campaign.

As the people prayed, President Trump was filled with the Holy Spirit and became so large that he looked like a giant balloon figure you see outside car dealerships.

He was much larger than life. He became unstoppable. His hands were raised to heaven in thanksgiving to God.

Dutch said to him, "Mr. President, you are the only thing standing between us and the hostile takeover of our nation by the radical left. You are giving us time to allow Holy Spirit to take our nation back into a great awakening. Thank you!"

The Ekklesia applauded and cheered.

INTERPRETATION:

In the dream, Dutch Sheets represents the Ekklesia and the prayer movement of our nation. The prophetic voices of America and the prayers of the Ekklesia are the only things keeping President Trump moving forward at this time in our nation. The weight of the responsibility and the constant attacks from the left and the media have deflated him. However, the prophetic decrees and intercession of God's Ekklesia are filling him up with the anointing and rejuvenating him as God's Cyrus in this hour.

DECREES

Father, in the name of Jesus, we decree that President Donald John Trump be filled with the Holy Spirit as your Cyrus to lead this nation out of bondage just as Cyrus lead Judah out of Babylon. We break the back of the attacks against him and silence the skeptics! Bring the words of the enemy against Trump to nothing, and expose the underlying enemy and hang him on his own gallows just as you did to Hayman. I thank you that you have raised up this man of God, President Donald John Trump, for such a time as this to lead our nation into a great awakening!

Oil for The Nation

Clay Nash

I had a dream that General McMaster (at the time, National Security Advisor to President Trump) requested a meeting with me. Upon entering the room, I noticed a man standing beside him that I assumed was from Israel.

General McMaster told me that he had one thousand tankers of 1,000-year-old olive oil from Israel. He asked if I could lead a movement to get boots on the ground to anoint the USA, fresh and new again.

When he finished speaking, the man with him told me the oil was not just a thousand years old but had been prayed over for a thousand years. As I stood in amazement of this vast this assignment, another person entered the room unannounced and spoke into General McMaster's ear.

General McMaster then spoke and asked if I had a background in crop-dusting. I said yes, my father had owned planes in my past and I ran the operation. General McMaster asked if could I rally crop-dusters to spray the USA with the oil. He assured me, "We will furnish all the oil they need to spray the nation."

I said, "Yessir, I can."

INTERPRETATION

In this dream, the 1,000 tankers of oil, 1,000 years old, prayed for over a period of 1000 years, speaks of a fresh Pentecost. We just celebrated the anniversary of Pentecost on May 29-31, 2020. This dream represents a fresh enduement of power.

General McMaster's question about anointing the nation through boots on ground referred to the Body of Christ carrying forth the new outpouring of the Spirit. His question about crop dusters was a reference to air superiority—the prayers of the church.

The fact that the oil came from Israel referred to our nation keeping our covenant Israel. They are praying for us, just as we pray for them.

DECREES

We declare a fresh enduement of power from on high for the body of Christ in our Nation.

We decree this new enduement of power will be facilitated by the Body of Christ becoming fitly joined and aligned together by what each joint supplies.

We declare that our covenant with Israel and their covenant with us is strong.

We declare that the number 1,000 speaks of endless supply, endless ages and endless prayers.

We thank you, Lord, for boots-on-the-ground healing our land and crop-duster air superiority.

We declare you have heard us, Lord. Send us answers so we can steward this new level of enduement of power with wisdom and strength at all times.

24 June 2020

Allegheny River

Clay Nash

I dreamed that President Donald *John the Beloved* Trump had a press conference to ask for intercession for a trip he was to take to the headwaters of the Allegheny River.

The day he made this trip, the praying church was lined on both banks to pray. Standing behind the praying church was the cloud of witnesses adding their agreement to the declarations and decrees being made by the praying church.

As President Trump traveled upstream in an open boat, Asian carp flew up from the river seeking to strike President Trump. As each carp surfaced, however, the body of faithful prayers declared and decreed protection over Trump. The carp were hit with flashes of bright light—

I felt they were Angels—and the fish were slammed back beneath the surface of the water.

When President Trump reached the headwaters, he began to decree about America completing its course and finishing well.

INTERPRETATION

This dream reveals that the prayers of the church and decrees and declarations of the Ekklesia are essential to provide protection to President Trump.

The presence of angels tells us that our prayers move spiritual armies—that we are not alone, but that the faith of the righteous activates God's provision for the President of the United States.

DECREES

We declare that the assignment coming out of any Asian nation will not prevail. Instead, it shall be pushed beneath the surface, not to resurface again.

We declare that the authority that George Washington gained and developed near this headwater location is being picked up again by President Trump.

We declare that the synergy of the praying church and the cloud of witnesses releases the new platform of power.

We stand in agreement with Heaven's will that President Trump will complete his mandated assignment and America will become an even great light to the world.

30 June 2020

Cobweb Spirit

Clay Nash

I dreamed that there was someone in Trump's administration who was standing behind him as he sat in his chair, and they would spray a cobweb on his head. It would cause him confusion.

Trump reached out to Dutch Sheets by paging 2222 (refer to the dream: "POTUS Request") and asking Dutch what he could do to free up his thinking and focus better.

Dutch told him he would contact Chuck Pierce for a sure word. Chuck told Dutch to tell President Trump he needed to be surrounded by praise and worship at all times.

I then saw a closet at the Whitehouse filled with cans of cobweb spray. These were like the silly string cans that kids play with. I saw a woman go and get one to spray on Trump but there was no aerosol in any of the cans.

INTERPRETATION

I stress that this dream does not represent an individual but a spirit of witchcraft and word curses.

The reference to Trump reaching out to Dutch is POTUS reaching out to spiritual authority. The 2222 number and pager refer back to the POTUS Request dream.

Dutch informing President Trump he would seek a sure word from the prophetic is again, the apostle and prophetic working together.

The answer of praise and worship speaks of them clearing the airways.

The closet being full speaks of decades and decades of evil having been given a place in that office.

The cans having no pressure or power speaks of praise and worship rendering the word curses powerless.

DECREES

We decree that President *John the Beloved* Trump will be surrounded by prayers, praise and worship at all times.

We declare every word spoken against POTUS will have no power.

We decree the Angels and Heavenly Host, along with the Body of Christ, will keep President Trump surrounded at all times with praise and worship.

We declare his focus will be sharp and his mind postured to hear Holy Spirit.

We declare the evil assignment against him as God's Cyrus to our nation is broken, cast down and destroyed.

111

We declare any person near him working as an evil agent will be removed... Now!

24 March 2018

Aircraft Carrier

<u>Clay Nash</u>

In the dream, I was watching a Fox News report. The announcer said, "Now we go to Jacksonville Florida for a live report on an unusual situation."

The onsite reporter was standing on the boardwalk of the St. John's River at the Cowford. It is the narrowest point of the river—the pinch point where cattlemen would ford the river with their cattle. It became the birthplace of a small village called Cow-ford that would later grow up to become Jacksonville, Florida.

The Fox News live reporter turned to point to an aircraft carrier filling up the entire river. It was stuck there. The reporter said, "The aircraft carrier, USS Gerald R. Ford, the largest aircraft carrier ever built, came up the St. John's River and got stuck in downtown Jacksonville."

The news anchor back in the studio asked, "Why would the carrier do that?"

The live reporter answered, "President Donald Trump sent the USS Gerald R. Ford up the river."

The news anchor was perplexed and asked, "Why would the President send America's largest aircraft carrier up the St. John's River? Wouldn't he know it would get stuck?"

The onsite reporter replied, "The President sent the aircraft carrier up the St. John's River because Dr. Don Lynch asked for it. The President says the carrier will remain here until Dr. Don Lynch says he is finished with it."

INTERPRETATION

I (Don Lynch) did not know Clay had the dream but I did know he would be joining us for the Sunday morning, "First Day Event," that our Kingdom Center has every Sunday morning. Clay and Dutch Sheets had been with us for the conference, and the conference was held in a completely different facility. The Sunday morning event was held at the location to which God had led us nine months before, on the boardwalk overlooking the St. John's River at the Cow-ford! Clay saw that place in the dream, awoke and came to it the next morning to find himself exactly where he was in the dream. He had never been to that location before the dream.

The aircraft carrier named Gerald R. Ford, is the largest carrier ever made. It is the launching table for God's Hornets. It is the tip of the spear. The name "Gerald" means "the rule of the spear." In real life, this aircraft carrier is home to the Screaming Eagles, the jets that take off and land on its deck. It was stuck on the ford or the narrowest part of the river called the Cow-ford.

In the dream, the aircraft carrier had been stuck at the narrowest point in the St. John's, where we were meeting and carrying on our warfare.

When Dutch Sheets stood up to preach, he said, "God informs me that He has now given us air superiority in this nation to change the judiciary."

DECREES

We declare that God has spiritual aircraft carriers being positioned so that prayers that are being brought boldly before the Throne of His grace will be heard and answers from Heaven will not be delayed.

We decree that the rule of God's sphere in the USA is increasing.

We decree that Screaming Eagles, God's Holy Convocation, are assembled and fueled for battle from their place of air superiority to allow answers with strategy to be received by the Ekklesia.

We declare that in this Apostolic Era of God's Kairos, the consistency of sending people forth to do the work of the ministry is increasing. We declare from that very place, the Cow-ford where innocent blood was shed by the Huguenots, a release of God's power in strength is going forth across the nation.

We decree people being saved, redeemed, made free, endued with power and commissioned to be the voice of righteous authority throughout America.

We decree that because our prayers are being heard and answers are being received, the turnaround of our Nation and the righteous markers of our fathers are being reset and reconstituted, establishing times of refreshing as promised by Father God.

We decree the piercing spear of God's word shall penetrate every heart across America.

We declare God is arising and our enemies are being scattered.

19 June 2020

Tsunami

Clay Nash

I dreamed that the top leaders of the church—the Generals of the Body of Christ—were standing facing the Atlantic Ocean. They were backed by people who were joined to their leadership roles. Behind them was the Cross of Cape Henry (a wooden cross erected by the early English settlers upon their safe arrival to Virginia in April of 1607).

One by one, these Generals stood up steadfast as the Cross backed their stand. There standing were Jane Hamon, Franklin Graham, Tony Perkins, Barbara Yoder, Harry Jackson Jr., TD Jakes, Dutch Sheets, Chuck Pierce, Cindy Jacobs, Billye Brim, Kenneth Copeland, Anthony Evans, Ramiro Pena, Paul Morton and many others, some I knew and countless others I did not know.

Behind them were millions of believers from all walks of life. They were gathered there as a result of a prophetic understanding that a Tsunami was coming to our nation.

As the tsunami came into sight, the command came from the leaders to raise our prayerful decrees for the tsunami to pass over those who had eyes to see and ears to hear. The Tsunami arrived as a total surprise to many but there were also those who were prepared to release Heaven's decree into the tsunami, not to stop it but to permeate it with Kingdom life and direct it to be as the wind that creates a threshing-floor effect (blowing away the chaff from wheat).

These decrees carried such a sound of heaven that the tsunami set some people who were crushed in fear, back to their stand in fresh hope and completed faith. Others who allowed themselves to be blinded by their fear and relaxed in their relationship with God were overwhelmed by the wave and swept out into the deep by a dark, unseen undertow.

Those who stood steadfast, however, having eyes of faith to see and ears fine-tuned to hear, used the tsunami to lift them to a higher platform of authority and purpose. They were released into a new flow of purpose that was secured by their willingness to trust God in this new level of greater authority.

The Generals began to give prophetic directives about prayer initiatives that would now secure their inheritances and establish God's original design for the nation.

The end of the dream came as a plane flew overhead with a banner attached:

"Look Vertical Not Horizontal
Answers Are On The Way."

The Generals then began a time of Praise for God's faithfulness and goodness.

Epilogue

Kingdom Voting Essential

on November 3, 2020

The upcoming November election will be proven in history as one of the most significant in our nation's history thus far. Yet many in the Body of Christ are far too passive regarding their stand in the political arena. Some have allowed the religious establishment to convince them their vote will make no difference. Some will just allow the busyness of life and their inability to plan ahead to cause them to not make it to the polls. In light of all who have great intentions, we must pray, plan and persevere to vote our conscience.

How should a follower of Jesus vote?

Allow me to share the wisdom on voting I have gained over my years as a Christian. Romans 14:17-18 states:

For the kingdom of God is not eating and drinking, but righteousness and peace and joy in the Holy Spirit. For he who in this way serves Christ is acceptable to God and approved by men.

To understand how to vote Kingdom as a follower of Jesus, we need a clear mindset focused on His Kingdom.

First, what is righteousness? When I have asked this question over the years, most answer "Right standing before God."

Yes, I agree with that, but I have grown to understand that righteousness is far greater than the ability to rightly stand before Father God. Righteousness is actually right relationship with God. Yes, you can rightly stand before someone by invitation but not necessarily have right relationship with that person. Righteousness, which is right relationship, only comes through repentance, and that always results in change.

CHANGE

To vote Kingdom, therefore, you must vote for those candidates who will initiate change. Not just any change, but change that produces a greater release of Kingdom life. When Kingdom life is released, established and flourishes, it crushes death. So, in voting righteously for change, we must ask: "Does this produce life for all?"

PEACE

Secondly, what is Kingdom peace and what releases that Kingdom peace internally within us? As I have rightly divided truth, I have concluded that my greatest time of peace is when my obedience is complete. We read in 2 Corinthians 10:5-6:

We are destroying speculations and every lofty thing raised up against the knowledge of God, and we are taking every thought captive to the obedience of Christ, and we are ready to punish all disobedience, whenever your obedience is complete.

Yes, my obedience—a righteous action—results in a peace that surpasses all understanding. So, in voting Kingdom, vote for those who will initiate and establish actions that produce internal peace and produce and establish life more abundantly. Life-producing actions result in change.

JOY

Finally, to vote Kingdom, you must vote for those who will establish greater joy in our nation. What brings about your greatest moments of joy? As I have asked this over the years, I have been given various answers. Many

126

get close to the proper answer but still miss the target. My greatest joy is experienced through my relationship with Jesus as Savior, Lord and King. Beyond that is my relationship with my wife Susan, my friend of over 50 years. Yes, Kingdom joy is experienced through righteous Kingdom relationships, thereby creating community.

In voting Kingdom, therefore, vote for those who will work to establish community and focus on working together, not those who are trying to divide and conquer we the people of this great nation—one that is destined to become greater.

Please pray, motivate others to pray, encourage others to get out and vote, and please vote for candidates who will initiate Kingdom actions, Kingdom change and Kingdom community.

Remember, God does not choose the perfect. He perfects His chosen.

About the Author

After becoming born again, Clay Nash yielded to the workings of Holy Spirit and began his journey to become a powerful prophetic voice to the Body of Christ. For almost 40 years now, he has traveled the world declaring the Kingdom of God in people's everyday lives. Out of his function as an Apostle, he has founded numerous assemblies of believers, maturing them to function as God's Ekklesia. He has also established a network of relational covenants with ministers throughout the world.

Clay serves on the team of Network Ekklesia International, led by Dutch Sheets. He also has the honor of being aligned with Chuck Pierce & Global Spheres. Clay has a doctorate in Theology.

Despite his many achievements, Clay's greatest accomplishment is that he has been married to Susan for over 45 years. Together they celebrate three wonderful adult children, four perfect grandchildren, along with numerous spiritual sons and daughters.

God has chosen to use Clay in the areas of signs & wonders, apostolic authority, prophetic direction & present-day truth from Godly wisdom. He and Susan have a deep passion for the body of Christ to inhabit their true purpose by discovering God's original intent.

They desire God's people to not only understand who they are in Christ, thus establishing their priestly anointing, but also knowing who Christ is in them, thus establishing their kingly authority. They know and live out this truth by being grounded in spiritual realities.

Some say Clay has no fear of taking chances, but that he carries a great concern of not taking chances. Some who know him well see his nature of being able to swoop down on a subject like an eagle with its talons flared. Many who have walked with him for years on his journey see the man that God is forming daily. Those who miss his surrendered heart, perhaps taking issue with his methods, may miss the fact that in some cases, the end justifies the means.

Those who have walked and worked with him closely, understand the madness of his divine interruptions. In the end, the grace that he carries brings melody to discord.

Yes, Clay Nash would rather open the bilge ports and sink the ship than sit idle and talk about what should be or could have been.

One of Clay's greatest strengths, causing his gaze to always be focused on the future horizon, is his understanding that God never works in our past, but He always works in our future.